ADVENTURES OF THE
"TIN-N-MAN"
AND HIS TRIP TO CANADA!

JOE KUREK

To order additional copies of this book, contact:
Xlibris
1-888-795-4274
www.Xlibris.com
Orders@Xlibris.com

The Tin-N- Man and his family own the Tin Bin Recycling Plant near Hunter's Creek, Florida.
It's located near Disney World and you can hear the rides and happy laughter of the Children who visit there every summer. It is a fun park, with rides, animals & fantastic goodies to eat and, of course, Ice Cream in every flavor imaginable, you just need to close your eyes and dream
of tasting so many wonderful flavors.

The Tin-N- Man lives with his brother Win Tin, in a mobile home made out of Silver Tin.

He has a dog named, Tin Rin !

And a cat named Tin Pin.

Everything in his home is made of Tin. Where does he get all that Tin?

4

From everyone who recycles those empty washed out pop cans, soup cans, coffee cans and even those empty tuna cans that you put into your blue boxes every week for the trash man to pick up.

Everyone loves a good tuna sandwich for lunch now and then. Maybe your mom packs one in your lunchbox for school once in a while.

The Tin Bin Recycling Plant only takes the metal tin containers that you put in your blue box, but the plastics go someplace else. Hunters Creek is near the alligator swamps in Florida and those mean critters go into the holding bins of tin that are waiting to be crushed and reused for tin. Those nasty alligators go after the dirty cans because they smell and still have food in them.

**So! Remember everyone you should wash your cans out so
they cannot be eaten by those nasty alligators.**

Remember ! Recycling is Good for the Environment !

There are a lot of different animals around Hunters Creek. You will find Deer, Rabbits, Mice, Giant Beetles, and those nasty alligators. Birds of all different varieties. In the ocean nearby you can find seals, and Sting Rays.

If you look hard you will see all these animals, birds and ocean dwellers in this picture!
<u>Look hard now, I'll just bet you can't find the mouse?</u>

Ha! Ha! He is sitting on the rabbits back!

The Tin-N-Man had his vacation time coming to him because it was July, in the middle of summer and all the families come to Florida with their children to visit Disney World, he wanted to go on a trip. At first, he thought of going to Mexico, but it is just as hot as Florida. When he put his metal thinking pan on his head he had a brilliant idea! Why not take a trip to CANADA!

The weather there is more pleasant and a bit cooler. He could drive his Tin Mobile, take Tin Rin and Tin Pin and pick up his friend "Triangle Eyes" on the way. First, he had to get the okay from his Brother Win Tin and his uncle Fin if they would take care of the Recycling Plant while he was gone. They told him to go ahead and have a fun time.

When the Tin-N-Man got home, he told Tin Rin and Tin Pin they were going on a trip.

Tin Rin ran around the house in circles jumping up and down and barking Ruff! Ruff! Arf! Tin Pin tried to jump on his shoulders and give him a lick, but slipped off his slippery tin. They both went nuts or should we say, "They went TIN".

They both sat by his legs when he picked up the phone and called his friend Triangle Eyes in Georgia.

Hello! Triangle Eyes, "Yes", This is the Tin-N-Man!

Before he could say anything else both Tin-Rin and Tin Pin went "TIN NUTS", they were jumping all around because they heard who he was talking to and both love Triangle Eyes.

Triangle Eyes, I've decided to go on a trip to CANADA and visit OTTAWA, Canada's Capital, but on the way, I want to also make a stop in WASHINGTON, D.C. and visit our UNITED STATES CAPITAL, to compare them! Would you like to join Tin Rin, Tin Pin and me? I need your EX-RAY TRIANGLE VISION, you can see for miles ahead and your computer brain can make all the metric conversions. Canadians use the European style of measurements for everything, we can talk more about it on the way.

"Yes", I would love to go on that trip", and I will join the three of you, but only if you keep those two animals away from jumping all over me! But, Triangle Eyes, you know they love you. Okay, I will pick you up tomorrow on the way in the Tin Mobile. "Okay!", See you in the afternoon! "Click".

Okay, you two it is all set! We leave in the morning after breakfast! We need a great start for the trip, milk and cereal. I will pack the Tin Mobile tonight. Once again Tin Rin and Tin Pin went " TIN NUTS". Ruff, Ruff, Ruff and Meow.

Off to bed, they all were dreaming of their trip to Canada with Triangle Eyes! The alarm went off in the morning and the Tin-N-Man prepared breakfast and they were off on their way to Georgia to pick up Triangle Eyes .

Tin Rin sat in the Front seat looking out the window and Tin Pin sat on the top of the back seat. The Ocean looked fantastic as they drove near the Florida Coast with so many boats and docks all against the beautiful blue sunlit skies and they finally made it to the Georgia Border.

Florida Coast

After a few more hours of driving they could pick up "Triangle Eyes" in Savannah. They needed to make a pit stop for lunch, and as it was so hot they also needed an ice cream treat.

"THAT HAS TO BE THE BIGGEST ICE CREAM STORE I HAVE EVER SEEN"

They finally made it to downtown, Savannah beeped the Tin Horn and out came "Triangle Eyes" with his bag.

He opened the door and you guessed it, Tin Rin and Tin Pin went nuts again, or should we say they went, "Tin Nuts" jumping all over "Triangle Eyes" but the Tin Man finally told them to settle down, because, he promised Triangle Eyes they would behave.

Triangle Eyes, got in the Tin Mobile and off they went heading North to Washington D.C. Tin-N-Man, I see you are dressed all casual for this trip and I like your green panned cap. You are usually in your work clothes at the Recycling Plant, when I visit you in Florida, said

Triangle Eyes.

THE TIN-N-MAN AND TRIANGLE EYES

Tin-N-Man, how come you are still not married?

Well, Triangle Eyes, I was seeing this nice lady but she was made from the plastic recycled items in the blue boxes, every time she gave me a hug, she would cut her arms on my Tin arms, she would touch the sharp pieces from the tops of tuna and soup cans. It just didn't work out, I did not want to hurt her anymore so we said goodbye.

I want to find a girl made all of Tin, just like myself! I want a girl with a large RED coffee can head and a YELLOW olive-oil cap that holds her eyes, mouth and nose just like mine. Red is the color of true love just like your heart. One day I will find her, I hope she has a pretty name.

Tin-N-Man, I am so sorry for you, but you still have Tin Rin and Tin Pin. (From the back seat came a Ruff, Ruff and a loud Meowww).

Oh! Look out the windows, they have such large tall bushy trees here in Georgia compared to Florida they are beautiful and everything is so green. Look at that Old Stump, 100 years old. This highway is so smooth and a scenic drive

Tin-N-Man, I have one more question for you! Why do you have the name Tin-N-Man? Why the big "N" in the middle?

Well, a long time ago in a place called OZ, there lived a YOUNG GIRL, a FRIENDLY LION and a TIN MAN. But that Tin Man, had a pointy head, eyes, nose and mouth. He was put together with rivets. If you look at me, "I'm AMERICAN MADE here in the United States". I have no rivets keeping me together. Just Look- No Holes!

I am put together with IMAGINATION and LOVE. The big "N" is for every can of TIN, that makes me who I am".

I think now it is time to stop, Tin Rin and Tin Pin have to take a walk and find a tree! They have to do their animal thing. Everybody back in, we are heading for South and North Carolina and on the way to Virginia.

THE WITCH'S FINGERS

They say Virginia is for lovers, but a long time ago a Nasty Witch lived there. You can only see her pointy fingers, as she is trying to pop open the sun.

Finally, we are almost in Washington D.C., what does D.C. mean, Triangle Eyes? It is the abbreviation for the District of Columbia. The United States has 50 States and the District of Columbia is where the President lives, and where Congress and the Senate conduct the business and most of the other offices that run our government. It is a city of Politics and Politicians who try to make the

United States function

LOOK OVER THERE the

Washington Monument!

Look over there! It's the Capital Building !

Over there is the White House where the President and his family live!

18

There is the "Arlington Cemetery". No, Tin Rin, we can't stop! No dogs allowed in there just Heroes have fought and died for our Country!

The District of Colombia is huge and it would take over a week to visit everything. Maybe, we could come back for another visit and look inside these places. I think now we should move on, but we need to have another pit stop first.

Look over there, an Art Gallery with a large parking lot, picnic tables, grass and trees. Okay, Tin Rin you and Tin Pin can go for a walk and have a drink. We can stop for some lunch, and there's a Hot Dog stand. Hot Dogs for everybody. Wow, yummy &

delicious, these foot long hot dogs really are!

Mustard, ketchup and relish in a soft bun and a drink of water and milk to chase it down. Close your eyes and imagine taking a bite! We have to always drink water to refresh our bodies.

Now Tin Rin and Tin Pin get back in the car to wait, I know your made of metal and the heat won't hurt you, while Triangle Eyes and I go into the Art Gallery to take a look. We will leave the windows down a little bit for you for fresh air.

"Triangle Eyes", this is interesting! WHAT IS IT?

It is called: "ABSTRACT ART". Take a look at the picture, it's named " FOUNDATIONS" and how the brickwork in the corner and over on the other side of it look like building blocks, just like the foundation in every house: "SOLID AS A ROCK".

Look at that one! Called, "THE BRIDGE", Tin-N-Man, I just love it! The peaks look just like my triangle eyes. You can see the bridge, with mixed colors going into the peaks!

Look over there! It is just like my eyes when I'm tired and is called:

"ARROWHEAD"

Over there's another one called: "BLACK RAIN" .

OKAY! Triangle Eyes, you have to explain that one! It is just as " KOOKY " as they come! Who ever heard of Black Rain? Well Tin-N-Man, it's like this. Maybe it just is too hard to paint Clear Rain, it is impossible we just cannot paint something that is clear!

If you would make it White Rain, what would it look like? SNOW, I guess!

What if you look up when it is raining, maybe you cannot see the black rain falling because your eyes will get all wet! But when you do finally see the rain it turns clear!

Maybe the artist, was just feeling sad and only saw black rain out of his eyes and painted it that way? Or maybe pollution turned it dark!

Triangle eyes, I GET IT! I GET IT! Abstract Art can be anything you want it to be. Yes! But some people just don't get it and they laugh.

We should never laugh at somebody else's art!

****

When you're in school, and the teacher tells you to draw in a coloring book, only some youngsters in the class can stay inside all the lines and make it life like. In the painting world, this could be called REALISM because it is perfect and looks so real.

Most youngsters, who try to paint inside the lines find their colors keep going outside the lines and they can be called IMPRESSIONISTS.

If you hold the coloring on the other side of the room, you cannot see the lines but you see how the colors look and create the picture that was drawn.

Finally, you have ABSTRACT ART. It can be anything you draw on a BLANK piece of paper. So, ONCE AGAIN we should never laugh at somebody's art, because it is what we see and feel about the picture that is important.

THAT WAS SOME ART CLASS!!! Good thing I brought you along, Triangle Eyes.

Now back to the Art Display, We have to Hurry!!! One last Painting, okay! Called, "Golden Web"

Okay! Tin-N-Man, we better head to the Tin Mobile and be on our way. Those animals have probably been barking and meowing at everybody walking by.

They finally are on their way in the Tin Mobile and heading toward Pennsylvania. Look at that BIG "P"!

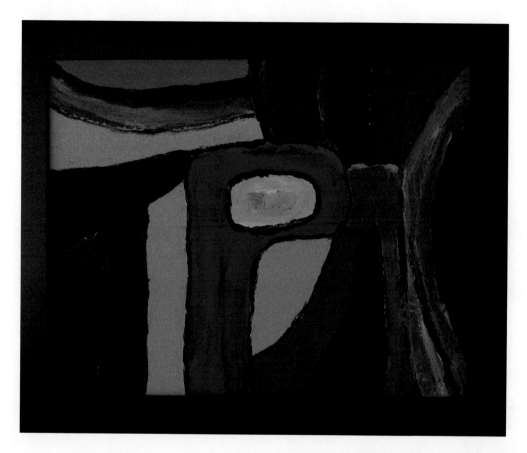

It's an Abstract Sign and must mean we are now in Pennsylvania. A few more hours and we will reach New York. Look at the peaks and down the Hill we go and look over there, "The Peak".

We are now almost out of Pennsylvania and into New York. Pennsylvania is full of mountains and hills. We are now almost out of Pennsylvania and here we come, "New York".

But which way do we go to get to CANADA? Lets go to Buffalo, we can see Niagara Falls and cross the Rainbow Bridge into Canada. Tin-N-Man, that sounds like a plan. I always wanted to see "NIAGARA FALLS".

"W O W". "SPECTACULARACIOUS" (a new word, can you say it?). Look at all that water! It helps make electricity for some of the homes in Canada and the United States.

GOSH! The Camera won't work! Batteries are out of juice. I can't take a picture, we will have to look on the Internet for a reminder!

Let's now head to Toronto, it is only a few hours away. They have funny money there called: "Loonies and Toonies". All the road distance signs are in kilometers. What is a kilometer, Triangle Eyes? Too complicated to address in this book we need to go to High School to learn that!

WOW! Toronto is huge, look at all those buildings! It almost scares me to drive here, as everybody keeps passing the Tin Mobile so fast.

We can take a few photos here in Toronto before we head to Ottawa, but we need to buy some fresh batteries. There should be some fantastic scenery on the way! I can't wait!

This map shows that the best road to take is Highway Number #7, as it goes all the way to OTTAWA. This is better as we are out in the country, no more fast cars here. Time for another pit stop, let's go for some burger's. "BURGER'S FOR EVERYBODY"! I want mine with ketchup, onions, relish and pickles! How about you guys?

There's a few trees over there, Tin Rin take Tin Pin for a walk. Be careful for POISON IVY! It is green and has three leaves together.

OKAY! Back in the car, we have three more hours to go to Ottawa, CANADA'S CAPITAL. Look at that bright sun and OH!

A Canadian Lake. So inviting, almost want to stop and take a Dip.

Tin-N-Man, that is just great, you have the camera working again. We need some better photos to show Uncle Fin and Win- Tin when we get back! Triangle Eyes, what do you see ahead with your X-ray Vision? I see a big metal sculpture on some rocks.

They look just like my eyes. We have to stop, it says:

"Studio 737 Art Gallery"

Another Art Gallery! Let's go in, it says: " Welcome to the Land O' Lakes Area"

This Art Gallery has only Original works and the owner says, it houses the largest collection of Original Canadian Art anywhere in Canada! WOW! Ottawa is only 2 hours away she mentions.

It has 10 full rooms of Art in every style. Over 1,000

ORIGINAL PAINTINGS. Triangle Eyes, let's go in that room. OKAY!

It looks just like the place we just passed down the road. Just beautiful, IMPRESSIONISTIC painting by the Gallery Owner, Arja Palonen. She has painted over 500 Paintings in her lifetime.

It's called: MADAWASKA FALLS by: Arja Palonen

See, I finally know all the differences in Art, it's just like an exam in school!

Look in the next room, it is all Abstract Art. I like this one. I just love all those colors together.

Let's take a picture of that fantastic sculpture before we leave for Ottawa! OKAY.

The Tin Blades look just like my, "Triangle Eyes". Take a good look, and compare and it is right here in Canada, not in Florida. They must Recycle in CANADA, just

like we do back home, to make something this beautiful. I think the big recycling plant is near Belleville.

32.

Let's give them a call when we are back in Florida! Everybody back in the Tin Mobile, we've got only 2 hours to go and we can see Canada's Parliament Buildings where the Canadian Government is run by the Canadian Politicians.

HOLY SMOKES! Ottawa is almost as big as Toronto. Look over there the Ottawa Parliament Building and the Ottawa River. Just Beautiful and Enormous!

Let's drive around to the other side, we need to see the front of the Parliament Building. So we can tell all of our friends about our trip.

They must have built that building over 150 years ago, it's made of stone and hardly no Tin?

OH! Look over there, another sculpture, it is:

Sir John Alexander MacDonald! He was Canada's First Prime Minister (That is the same as our American President's role)

Oh! Our trip is now complete and time to head back home! I hope everybody reading about our trip had a good time and learned a few things. Just what did you learn on this trip?

Perhaps, Everybody will be waiting for the Tin-N-Man, Tin Rin, Tin Pin and Triangle Eyes to go on another Adventure. Would you like to come with them? Maybe we can even come back to Canada, everyone is so Friendly!

GOODBYE FOR NOW! SEE YOU SOON!

Printed in the United States
By Bookmasters